Endorsements

A poignant text of history and hope told through the stories of women who have left footprints for other women to follow as others follow them. This book is a must-read for those who want to aspire higher and lead from wherever they are as they take women to the destiny they must fulfill.

Dr. Sabrina D. Black

Counselor, International Speaker, Human Rights Advocate, and Author of "Help for Your Leadership," "Live Right Now," and "Can Two Walk Together."

As an advocate for women's empowerment, I highly recommend "The Gift of Women." This book shines a much-needed light on the ongoing inequities women still face worldwide and the impact these disparities have on the global community. With a message of hope and a call to action, this book challenges women to live boldly and bravely, to erase the commentary of those who have said they are not enough or less than others, and to embrace their God-given gifts and destinies.

A powerful reminder that women everywhere have the power to make a difference, no matter their station in life. It encourages women to dream big, pursue their goals, and fight for the freedom and justice we all deserve. This book is a timely reminder of women's vital role in shaping our world and the legacy we leave for future generations.

Melissa McCrery

Founder, The Higher View Nation of Women

Women who have gone before paved the way for young leaders like me to have an education, a voice, and an impact in my community and to contribute to the development of the next generation of women to come.

Ruth Nyaleel Kai Thoat
Founder and Executive Director
African Indigenous Women Empowerment
Juba, South Sudan

An enlightening read which describes inspiring historical agents of change, highlights the current plight of women in the developing world, and presents practical solutions to age-old problems.

Mary Dailey Brown
President, Sow Hope

Inspiring and practical information about the past, present, and future education of women, this book explains the difficulties facing impoverished, disenfranchised women in becoming all that God has made them to be.

Dr. Diane Davis
Academic Dean, Aletheia Christian College

An holistic empowerment of the sisterhood of girls and women is the pursuit for all who seek a prosperous society. The themes in this book offer hope for the future.

Elisama W Daniel
Executive Director, ACROSS

The Gift of Women

TERESA JANZEN

&

THERESA WILLEN

She opens her mouth with wisdom,
and the teaching of kindness is on her tongue.

Proverbs 31:26

The Gift of Women

TERESA JANZEN &
THERESA WILLEN

FOREWORD BY DR. SABRINA D. BLACK

Abundance Books

The Gift of Women

ISBN: 979-8-9857499-7-7 (Print)
ISBN: 979-8-9857499-8-4 (eBook)

Published by Abundance Books, LLC
417 Forest St., Suite 445
Kalamazoo, MI 49001

abundance-books.com

The book, "Dreams" is public domain. Written by Olive Schreiner in 1890.

"A Mother's Day Proclamation" is public domain. Written by Julia Ward Howe in 1870.

Unless otherwise indicated, all scripture is taken from the ESV® Bible (The Holy Bible, English Standard Version®), copyright © 2001 Crossway, a publishing ministry of Good News Publishers. Used by permission. All rights reserved.

Foreword by Dr. Sabrina D. Black

Edited and Cover Design by Theresa Willen

Printed in the USA

Table of Contents

Foreword

The authors of these words empower women to know that regardless of their journey and because of that journey there are women looking up to and following them. Each woman may have forged her own path, but there is a road that leads to greatness that has already been established, and you, my sisters, can illuminate the path for those who are yet to take the journey. The dream that Oliver Shriner talks about in his book is symbolic of the visions that many women have had. At some level, we have questioned who we are, our existence, value, and destiny.

As women begin to live an unedited life and return to the original glory in which they were created, knowing that they have been wonderfully and fearfully made, they will begin to walk boldly and bravely into all the future holds for them. To live unedited is to erase the commentary and voices of those around you who have said you are too much or not enough (not tall enough, pretty enough, rich enough, smart enough, and the list goes on). This text unties the proverbial knots and declares to women that enough is enough. Whatever they have, the Lord has provided and can use women the way they are now, even as they become who they will be as a voice to the nations.

This text gives hope to those women around the world who have been marginalized. Women who are vulnerable. God sees, and He knows. He is shining a light on their plight and bringing to the forefront the numerous injustices women have endured.

As a global humanitarian and African American missionary for almost 40 years, I traveled throughout the world to over 70 different countries. I have witnessed women in high places and those who are of a low estate in the caste system. No matter their life station, women still dream and have visions. They have hopes and desires for their family, their community, and themselves. Many of their dreams are hindered by the limitations of the societies in which they dwell. This book allows them to be free in their minds and motivates them to create freedom within the systems to which they are bound. Every woman who fights for freedom makes it easier for the next woman. As we gather together during International Women's Month, we call on our sisters from every walk of life to walk toward the future and continue to carry the torch that lights the way.

Women have and do make a difference. This text highlights only a few of the many contributors to world change and their contributions. Their names and stories are part of your legacy, your heritage. As you see the markers of their footprints, know that other women also see yours. Lead well, my sisters, in the area of life where we need you most: EVERYWHERE! We are the nation.

Dr. Sabrina D. Black, Author, Counselor, Professor, International Speaker, Global Humanitarian and Missionary
www.drsabrina.net

Introduction

In Olive Schreiner's book, *Dreams* (1890), a woman journeys to the Land of Freedom and along the way she meets old man Reason at the steep bank of a river.

And Reason, that old man, said to her, "Silence! What do you hear?"

And she listened intently, and she said, "I hear a sound of feet, a thousand times ten thousand and thousands of thousands, and they beat this way!"

He said, "They are the feet of those that shall follow you. Lead on! make a track to the water's edge! Where you stand now, the ground will be beaten flat by ten thousand times ten thousand feet." And he said, "Have you seen the locusts how they cross a stream? First one comes down to the water-edge, and it is swept away, and then another comes and then another, and then another, and at last with their bodies piled up a bridge is built and the rest pass over."

She said, "And, of those that come first, some are swept away, and are heard of no more; their bodies do not even build the bridge?"

"And are swept away, and are heard of no more—and what of that?" he said.

"And what of that—" she said.

"They make a track to the water's edge."

1

"They make a track to the water's edge—." And she said, "Over that bridge which shall be built with our bodies, who will pass?"

He said, "The entire human race."

And the woman grasped her staff.

And I saw her turn down that dark path to the river.

Just as the woman in Schreiner's dream faced the dark and dangerous river for the sake of those who would follow, countless women have suffered and sacrificed to forge a path for those who would come after them. It was not for their own benefit that they risked so much, but for ours. In their footsteps, we humbly continue the journey toward a more equitable society for women and girls worldwide.

Equality is a fundamental human right enshrined in various international declarations, conventions, and treaties, yet roughly half the population may be marginalized because of gender. While not all women experience marginalization, the vast majority have, and do, experience some degree of inequity. In the developing world, many women and girls struggle to access even the most basic human rights simply because they were born female.

Marginalized people are outside of the mainstream of society and lack access to the resources and opportunities most people take for granted. They may be excluded from political, economic, social, or cultural participation. They may face discrimination, poverty, and other forms of social injustice. Marginalized people can include various groups, such as ethnic and racial minorities, indigenous people, people with disabilities, refugees and asylum seekers, and people living in poverty. A unique factor for women and girls is that they may be marginalized based on gender, but they are also often members of these other socially side-lined groups—making them even more vulnerable.

Overview of Issues

The experience of marginalization can vary depending on factors such as location, culture, and social context and can significantly impact the health and well-being of individuals and communities. For women and girls in the developing world today, issues may vary from region to region and even within individual countries; however, common themes emerge: access to education, economic empowerment, access to healthcare, gender-based violence, political representation, and access to technology. We will examine the impact of women leaders on women's development to draw inspiration and hope among the sisterhood of women and girls around the world.

Access to Education
Despite significant progress in recent years, many girls and women around the world still face significant barriers to education. This can include everything from a lack of funding for schools and teachers to cultural attitudes prioritizing boys' education over girls. Without access to education, girls, and women may struggle to gain the skills and knowledge needed to secure good jobs and fully participate in society.

Economic Empowerment

Women in developing countries often face significant economic challenges, including low wages, limited job opportunities, and a lack of access to credit and other resources needed to start their own businesses. This can leave them vulnerable to poverty and exploitation, making supporting themselves and their families difficult.

Access to Healthcare

Women in many parts of the world still lack access to basic healthcare services, including prenatal care, childbirth support, and family planning resources. This can seriously affect maternal and child health and limit women's ability to participate fully in their communities and economies.

Gender-based Violence

Women in many parts of the world face significant threats of violence, including physical and sexual assault, domestic abuse, and human trafficking. These threats can limit women's ability to move freely and participate in society and can have lasting physical and psychological consequences.

Political Representation

Despite progress in recent years, women are still significantly underrepresented in many areas of public life, including politics. This can limit their ability to shape policies and laws that affect their lives and can perpetuate gender inequalities.

Access to Technology

While technology has the potential to be a powerful tool for women's empowerment, it can also perpetuate existing inequalities. Women in many parts of the world still lack access to the internet and other digital tools and may face significant barriers to using technology to access education, find employment, and participate in their communities.

- 1-

Forging a Path

While we acknowledge the challenges facing women and girls today, we would be remiss to ignore the drastic progress made in the past 200 years, particularly in the areas of education, healthcare, and economic empowerment. While there is still room for improvement, a foundation in these critical areas has launched a global movement of women supporting the development of other women—abroad and within their own communities.

We have seen significant educational changes for women and girls, with progress varying depending on geographic location, cultural norms, and socio-economic factors. According to the World Bank, in the early 19th century, less than 1% of the world's female population had access to education. By the early 21st century, this had risen to over 90% in many countries. The global literacy rate for women was just 25% in 1800, and according to UNESCO, despite the overall rise in literacy rates worldwide, most illiterate adults today are women.

Similarly, changes in healthcare for women in the last 200 years have been significant. There has been a greater emphasis on women's health issues, including gender-specific illnesses and reproductive health. Maternal mortality rates have decreased due in part to better healthcare for pregnant women and new mothers. Improvements in child health and access to medical facilities have also led to decreased child mortality rates. The development of new medical technologies, such as vaccines, antibiotics, and diagnostic tools, has greatly improved women's health outcomes. For example, vaccines have virtually eliminated diseases like smallpox and polio, and antibiotics have greatly reduced infection and mortality rates. In many parts of the world, women now have better access to healthcare services than they did in the past. This includes access to medical facilities, trained healthcare providers, and medications.

The combined improvements to education and health services for women have also set the stage for broadening economic opportunities. While women still struggle more than their male counterparts to access lines of credit and legal services, the opportunities for grassroots and cottage industries are more diversified than in the previous century.

While there are many factors to which we can credit these recent improvements, one often overlooked and sometimes controversial influence is the impact of female foreigners who entered the developing world with the influx of church-sponsored missionaries in the 19th and 20th centuries. How is it that these women were able to influence culture and pave the way for the betterment of their marginalized sisters when they, too, faced gender obstacles in both their homeland and their field of service?

Much can be said, both positive and negative, about the impact of foreign missionaries, but for the purpose of this writing, we will choose to look specifically at the contributions made by female foreigners and ask ourselves if their pioneering work may have laid a foundation for those who came later. I (Teresa

Janzen) can only observe from my own perspective as a contemporary female foreign developmental missionary.

I moved to South Sudan in 2016 for the purpose of re-opening a village school and working with women in the area of economic empowerment. In my early months in the country, I would find myself the lone woman amidst groups of men. On one such occasion, at a male friend's wedding, I asked a colleague, "where are the women? Shouldn't I be with them?"

"No," he responded. "You are not like our women."

I have often thought about that statement with a twinge of loneliness. However, what makes me *not a local woman* is also what may have allowed foreign female missionaries to introduce ideas and influence in a male-dominated society on behalf of her local sister. The foreign woman can advocate for those whose voice may not otherwise be heard because she is viewed differently by the men in the culture. While it is imperative that women in development forge female friendships in the kitchens and around the craft tables of the ladies they serve, it is equally important that they gain the trust of the men in the community. In this way, they carve a path through the jungle of ignorance for other women to follow and further.

Historic Heroines

Many women have entered foreign service through both the church and humanitarian systems. In recent years, women out-number men in missionary service almost 2:1 (Pioneers, 2022). While many changes are happening regarding the relevance and role of foreign missionaries in the developing world, let's pause to recognize just a few of the women who have beaten a path toward the river.

Ann Hasseltine and Sarah Boardman:
One of the first female protestant missionaries was Ann Hasseltine. Though some sources credit her as the first single woman to brave the rigors of the foreign mission field, Miss Hasseltine met and married Adoniram Judson while en route to serve in Burma (now Myanmar) (Knowles, 1846). Ann Judson learned the Burmese language and strove to improve access to education until her untimely death in 1826 at the age of 36. Her work, however, didn't stop. Within a year, Reverend Judson married the recently widowed Sarah Boardman, who had served in Burma with her late husband (Judson, 1860). In the face of enormous challenges, including times of imprisonment and torture, Sarah continued to work in the educational arena and is especially known for making education accessible to Burmese women and girls. Illness forced Sarah to return to America, but she died en route in 1845 at the age of forty-two. Her work continues through The American Baptist International Ministries (IM), which continues to work in the areas of health and education in Myanmar.

Betsey Stockton:
In 1821, Betsey Stockton became the first single-woman missionary of the modern mission movement (Hildreth, 2019). Starting as a domestic slave, she took evening classes at the College of New Jersey, now Princeton University. Through a new program of gradual emancipation, Betsey became the paid servant of Ashbel Green, the president of Princeton University.

Her education was supported and sponsored by tutoring and the use of the library in the household. Ashbel's letter of recommendation landed Betsey with the American Board of Commissioners for Foreign Missions (ABCFM). Betsey answered God's call to take the Gospel to those who had never heard it. She gained her freedom and was commissioned and sent to the Sandwich Islands (today Hawaii) as the only black person on a team of eleven. Throughout her life, she shared the love of Christ and passed along the gift of education to thousands of students.

Lottie Moon

Lottie Moon is another female Christian missionary who significantly impacted the world. Born in Virginia in 1840, she began her missionary work in China in 1873 (Schrock, 2014). Lottie's work focused on promoting women's education and advocating for the rights of the Chinese people during a time of political unrest. She recognized the importance of education in empowering women and improving their lives. Lottie worked to establish schools and promote literacy among girls and women in China, a task that was often met with significant resistance. Her advocacy for the Chinese people during a time of political unrest also helped to bring attention to the struggles of the Chinese people and raise awareness of the need for change.

Mary Slessor

Mary Slessor was born in Scotland in 1848 and began her missionary work in Calabar (now part of Nigeria) in 1876 (Mueller, 1941). She spent the next thirty-eight years working to promote education and healthcare in the region, often in the face of significant opposition. Mary is perhaps best known for her advocacy for the rights of women and children in Africa and for condemning the practice of infanticide of twin babies. She worked to promote education for girls, recognizing that education was a critical tool for empowering women and improving their lives. Through her work, Mary helped pave the way for a brighter future for countless women and children in Africa. Her legacy inspires others to work for the betterment of all people, regardless of their background or circumstances.

Mother Teresa

One of the most well-known female Christian missionaries is Mother Teresa. Born in Albania in 1910, she joined the Sisters of Loreto at the age of 18 and began her missionary work in India in 1929. In 1950, she founded the Missionaries of Charity, a religious order dedicated to serving the poorest of the poor (Pettinger, 2019). The order operates schools, orphanages, and clinics worldwide, providing much-needed services to those in need. Mother Teresa's work has had a profound impact on the world. She is widely recognized as a champion of the poor and an advocate for those who are often overlooked by society. Her work has inspired countless others to take up the causes of social justice and economic empowerment of the most marginalized worldwide and serve the less fortunate in their communities.

Elizabeth Elliot

A final example of historical female heroines is Elisabeth Elliot, a notable female Christian missionary who significantly impacted the world. Born in Belgium in 1926, she began her missionary work in Ecuador in 1952 (Littlewood, 2022). Elizabeth's work focused on promoting the Christian faith and advocating for the rights of indigenous peoples in South America. She helped to bring attention to the struggles of the indigenous peoples in South America, who were often marginalized and oppressed by the dominant cultures. She advocated for their rights and worked to establish a sense of dignity and respect for their unique cultures and traditions.

Elizabeth Elliot is perhaps best known for her work in the aftermath of the deaths of her husband and four other missionaries, who were killed by members of the Waodani tribe in 1956. Following this tragedy, Elizabeth remained committed to her work and continued to live among the Waodani, eventually helping to reconcile the tribe and the families of the slain missionaries. Elizabeth demonstrated a deep commitment to serving others and promoting the values of the Christian faith. Her legacy inspires others to work for social justice and build bridges between different cultures and communities.

Despite many challenges, countless women have persisted in their efforts to serve as missionaries and development workers and have made significant contributions in improving the lives of women and girls in the developing world. Their work has challenged gender stereotypes and created a more inclusive and equitable vision of their communities and the world. They have battled the church and culture to enter a male-dominated workplace in harsh and foreign lands. They have learned languages, adapted to different customs, and braved all kinds of travel to serve their global sisters in a way a male missionary or development worker never could. The female voice of the foreign missionary has led to the amplified voice of local women in the developing world whose time has now arrived.

- 2 -

Contemporary Voices

Today, women from around the world continue the work of women's empowerment with a new emphasis in areas such as business, social justice, human rights, and leadership. In addition to the continuing efforts of foreign missionaries, many women serve their own communities through the church, business, and humanitarian sectors. The time for new voices is now. With the support of the global sisterhood and local women leaders, women are using their voices and taking their place like never before.

Canon Hilda Kabia

Canon Hilda Kabia is a Kenyan Anglican priest and a leading figure in the Anglican Church in Kenya (Macdonald, 2018). She was born in 1965 in Murang'a County, Kenya. After completing her primary and secondary education in Kenya, she went to Uganda for her tertiary education, where she studied at Makerere University and received a degree in psychology. After completing her studies, Kabia worked as a community development worker for several years. During this time, she was involved in various community development projects, including promoting health and sanitation, education, and empowerment of women and girls. Kabia later felt called to ministry and enrolled at St. Paul's University in Limuru, Kenya, where she studied theology. She was ordained a deacon in 1996 and a priest in 1997, becoming one of the first women to be ordained in the Anglican Church of Kenya.

Kabia has held various leadership positions in the church. She served as a chaplain at the University of Nairobi and the Kenya Institute of Management before being appointed as the first woman canon in the Anglican Church of Kenya in 2002. She served as the Provincial Secretary for Gender and Family Affairs for the Anglican Church of Kenya from 2008 to 2016, and was appointed as the first female principal of Msalato Theological College in Tanzania.

A strong advocate for gender equality and the empowerment of women and girls, Kabia has been involved in various initiatives to promote women's leadership and participation in the church and society. In 2011, she co-founded the Women's Guild of the Anglican Church of Kenya, which provides a platform for women to participate in the church's decision-making processes and to promote gender equality in the church and society. Kabia has also been involved in various community development projects, including providing education and vocational training to women and girls, promoting health and sanitation, and advocating for the rights of women and girls. She is a member of various organizations and networks working on women's empowerment, including the Kenya Women's Political Caucus and the African Women's Development and Communication Network.

Kabia's work has been recognized both nationally and internationally. In 2014, she was awarded the Order of the Grand Warrior by the President of Kenya in recognition of her contribution to women's empowerment and community development. In 2015, she was appointed to the United Nations Commission on the Status of Women, where she represented the Anglican Communion.

Dr. Sabrina Diana Black

A human rights activist and modern-day abolitionist, Dr. Sabrina Diana Black founded Global Projects in 2003 after serving in the foreign mission field under male leadership for eighteen years. Global Projects provides hope, help, and healing for underserved and underprivileged girls and women around the world.

A trailblazer in higher education, Dr. Black has been a professor at numerous colleges and seminaries, including Grace College, Ashland Theological Seminary, and Moody Theological Seminary. She has established several global programs to address the need for education, STEM, and leadership: Girls with Great Potential, Phenomenal Women's Conference, Women Who Lead and Aspire Hire: Leadership Think Tank. Over the years, with service in various parts of Africa, the UK, Bulgaria, Romania, Budapest, and Mongolia, Dr. Black has provided counseling, crisis intervention, and trauma training for victims of sexual assault and human trafficking. Dr. Black began her work in the area of human rights in 2005 at the Winter Olympics in Turino, Italy. She has provided trafficking education and awareness in schools, churches, and for organizations, in addition to serving with the Michigan Rescue and Restore Coalition and as an Appointee for the National Juneteenth Sex Trafficking Commission. She has received numerous awards and honors for her work, including Teacher of Excellence Award, Top 100 Educators, Kingdom Dreamer Award for Global Outreach, Community Icon Award, Destiny Award for Global Outreach, Spirit of Detroit Award, Who's

Who in Black Detroit, The Great Commission Humanitarian of the Year Award and the Global Impact Award. She also won the Herald Award for Journalism and for Radio Broadcasting.

In 1985 when Dr. Sabrina Black first went to Uganda, she was unknowingly following in the footsteps of Betsey Stockton and others who took color to the mission field. For several years, and in many African countries, Dr. Black was considered the Biblical Joseph who was from the American promised land, returning home to provide relief to her sisters and brothers and reminding them of their royal heritage in Christ.

Dr. Mae Elise Cannon

Based in North America, Dr. Mae Elise Cannon is a well-known Christian advocate and leader dedicated to serving marginalized communities and promoting justice and peace worldwide. She is the Executive Director of Churches for Middle East Peace (CMEP), an organization that works to encourage US policies that promote peace and justice in the Middle East. She is also the author of several books, including "Social Justice Handbook: Small Steps for a Better World," which has become a key resource for individuals and organizations seeking to engage in social justice work (Cannon, 2020).

Dr. Cannon is an ordained minister in the Evangelical Covenant Church and has served in various ministry roles throughout her career. She received her Ph.D. in American History from the University of California, Davis, and has taught at several universities, including North Park University and Bethel University. She has also served as the pastor of Hillside Covenant Church in Walnut Creek, California.

One of Dr. Cannon's most notable contributions to Christian community development is her work on peacebuilding in the Middle East. As the Executive Director of CMEP, she has been a leading advocate for US policies that promote a just and peaceful resolution to the Israeli-Palestinian conflict. She has worked to mobilize Christians nationwide to engage in advocacy efforts and has been a frequent speaker on the topic at conferences and events.

Dr. Cannon has also been a prominent voice on race and social justice issues in the Christian community. In her book, "Social Justice Handbook," she provides practical guidance for individuals and churches seeking to engage in social justice work, focusing on issues of race and privilege.

Dr. Cannon's work has been recognized and celebrated by many organizations and individuals within the Christian community. She has received numerous awards and honors for her contributions to Christian community development, including the 2014 Distinguished Alumnus Award from North Park University and the 2016 Gordon-Conwell Theological Seminary Alumnus of the Year Award.

Nalini M Jayasuriya
Prof. Nalini M Jayasuriya was an internationally acclaimed artist from Sri Lanka. She has exhibited her soul-stirring paintings throughout the world: Manila, London, Bangkok, Paris, Toronto, Tokyo, Jerusalem, and New York (Finlayson, 2021). Born in Colombo in 1954, Jayasuriya studied at the University of Kelaniya in Sri Lanka, where she completed her Bachelor of Arts degree in 1975, followed by her Master of Fine Arts degree in 1982. She later obtained her Doctor of

Philosophy in Art Education from the University of Illinois at Urbana-Champaign in the United States.

Nalini started her career as a teacher at St. Thomas College Mount Lavinia, Sri Lanka. She was awarded Sri Lanka's highest honor for the Arts by the Government of Sri Lanka. Numerous books featuring her paintings and her poetry have been published in several languages. Nalini taught art history and music history at various universities in seven different countries, including Yale University in New Haven, Connecticut, an alma mater.

While Nalini passed away in September 2014, the culture-challenging work of her art continues. She saw herself as a historian and interpreted her art from an Asian Christian perspective. Overall, Prof. Nalini M. Jayasuriya's art and activism have significantly impacted the contemporary art scene in Sri Lanka and beyond. Her work is a powerful reflection of the complex social, cultural, and political issues that continue to shape our world today.

Dr. Alveda King
The niece of Martin Luther King Jr. and daughter of activists Rev. A. D. King and Naomi Ruth Barber King, Dr. Alveda King is an American minister, civil rights activist, and author known for advocating pro-life and conservative political views. Dr. King grew up in the civil rights movement, experiencing first-hand the struggles and successes of the movement. Her involvement in the civil rights movement began when she was just a child, marching with her family and attending rallies with her uncle Martin Luther King Jr. She witnessed the 1963 March on Washington, where her uncle delivered his famous "I Have a

Dream" speech, and also the 1965 Selma to Montgomery march.

In the early 1970s, Dr. Alveda King became involved in the pro-life movement, which advocates for the rights of the unborn. She had two abortions herself before becoming a pro-life advocate, and she has since dedicated her life to promoting pro-life policies and speaking out against abortion. She is a frequent speaker at pro-life events and has written several books on the subject.

In addition to her work as a minister and pro-life advocate, Dr. Alveda King is also involved in politics. She has supported conservative political causes and served as a Georgia State House of Representatives member. Dr. Alveda King has received numerous awards and recognitions for her work, including the Life Prize Award from the Gerard Health Foundation in 2011, the Civil Rights Award from Congress of Racial Equality (CORE) in 2012, and the Pro-life Recognition Award from the 40th Annual National Right to Life Convention in 2013.

Throughout her life, Dr. Alveda King has been a powerful voice for civil rights, pro-life activism, and conservative politics. Her dedication to these causes has inspired many and made a lasting impact on American society.

Heidi Baker

Heidi Baker is a contemporary Christian missionary and author who has spent much of her life serving in Mozambique. Baker's faith journey began at the age of 16 when she heard a Navajo evangelist preach. She earned a Bachelor's degree in Christian

Education from Vanguard University in Southern California, a Master's degree in Biblical Studies from the same institution, and a Ph.D. in Systematic Theology from King's College, University of London.

In 1980, Baker and her husband, Rolland, moved to Mozambique to work as missionaries. They established Iris Global ministry in 1983, and it has since become a major Christian humanitarian organization. Baker's ministry has focused on serving Mozambique's poor, orphaned, and widowed. She and her husband have founded schools, churches, and medical clinics throughout the country and have also established a network of more than 5,000 churches in various parts of Africa. Baker has also authored several books on her experiences in Mozambique and her faith journey, including "Compelled by Love" and "Birthing the Miraculous."

One of the hallmarks of Baker's ministry has been her focus on "signs and wonders." She believes that God is still working miracles today and has witnessed many instances of divine healing, supernatural provision, and other remarkable occurrences. She helps equip western missionaries to minister cross-culturally and serve in various contexts around the world.

In addition to her ministry work in Mozambique, Baker has also been involved in relief efforts in other parts of the world. She has traveled to countries such as India and China to serve the poor and has spoken out on issues such as human trafficking and the persecution of Christians. Baker has been recognized for her humanitarian work with numerous awards and honors, including the Mother Teresa Memorial Award for Social Justice in 2010 and the Order of Merit from the Mozambican government in 2018. She continues to serve in Mozambique and worldwide, inspiring others with her message of faith, love, and compassion.

- 3-

Continuing Inequities

While many individuals and organizations have worked for improvements in equitable opportunities for women and girls, there continues to be challenges in all areas previously mentioned. Education, however, is one area with not only great challenges, but also incredible opportunity. Through improved access to quality education, women will continue to take an increasing role in developing their communities and the world.

Although progress has been made in reducing the gender gap in education overall, there is still a significant gender gap in science, technology, engineering, and math (STEM) fields. According to UNESCO, women and girls are still underrepresented in STEM education, with girls making up just 35% of students enrolled in STEM-related subjects at the tertiary level.

Even when women make a mark in history, it is often not noted, as in the case of Katherine Johnson, who was the epitome of STEM. At the age of 15, this little black girl was already in college studying science, technology, engineering, and math. She and her colleagues, Mary Jackson and Dorothy Vaughn, represented a portion of women's history that many did not know. They came to the forefront because of the dramatization of "Hidden Figures." These African American women were mathematicians referred to as computers (because they computed and calculated the numbers that were associated with physics and orbital mechanics). They made a major impact in the space race and helped NASA launch a man to the moon.

Despite increased access to education, the quality of education for women and girls remains a challenge in many parts of the world. According to the UN, 130 million girls aged 6-17 are out of school, with many facing barriers such as poverty, child marriage, and discrimination.

While women make up a significant proportion of the teaching workforce, they are still underrepresented in leadership roles in education. According to UNESCO, just 28% of tertiary education management positions are held by women.

In the developed world, women now outnumber men in tertiary education, yet women still face barriers to accessing higher education in the majority world. In sub-Saharan Africa, for example, The World Bank reports that just 8% of women aged 25 and over have completed tertiary education, compared to 12% of men.

Despite progress in many areas, there are still countries where girls have limited access to education. Some of the countries that are lagging the most in girl child education include:

Afghanistan
Afghanistan remains one of the worst countries in the world for girls' education. Only 37% of girls are literate, and only about a third of girls are enrolled in primary school. Sometimes, women and girls cannot leave their homes without a male family member present.

Pakistan

In Pakistan, there are significant educational disparities between boys and girls, with girls often facing discrimination and violence. While the country has made progress in recent years, with a 30% increase in girls' enrollment in primary school, many girls still do not attend school, especially in rural areas.

Yemen

Yemen is one of the poorest countries in the Middle East, and the ongoing civil war has made the situation even more difficult for girls. Only about 36% of girls attend primary school, and the dropout rate is high.

Nigeria

While Nigeria has made progress in improving access to education for girls, there are still significant barriers. In the northern part of the country, where poverty is widespread, many girls are forced to drop out of school early to help support their families.

South Sudan

South Sudan has one of the lowest literacy rates in the world, with only 27% of the population able to read and write. Girls are especially affected, with only about 16% of girls attending primary school.

Overall, there has been significant progress in education for women and girls in the last 200 years, with increased access to education and improved literacy rates. However, there is still work to be done to ensure that women and girls have equal access to quality education and are represented in leadership roles as we enter the digital age.

- 4 -

Education in the Digital Age

The development of gender equality and self-efficacy in women is the main focus of the fifth of seventeen Sustainable Development Goals established by the United Nations in 2015. The deadline to achieve these goals was initially set to 2030, but because of the pandemic and other mitigating factors, "progress on gender equality has not only failed to move forward but has begun to reverse" (UN Women, 2022). Getting back on track is paramount for women's empowerment. Social, political, economic, and psychological have all "played a pivotal role in strengthening and empowering women in every society" (Al-Rashdi & Abdelwahed, 2022). This empowerment plays out differently in different national cultures, and it would be presumptuous to have a one-size-fits-all approach to empowering women around the globe. However, some constants can be established. For example, in 2022, "of women and girls aged 15-49, more than one in 10 (12.5%) were subjected to sexual and/or physical violence by an intimate partner in the last year" (UN Women, 2022). This, of course, is unacceptable and is a non-negotiable regarding women's self-efficacy. Additionally, child marriage "can [harm] women's reproductive health, access to education, relative bargaining position within the family and ... [lead to] domestic violence" (Advancing gender, 2019). Both of these examples give rise to the belief that men are at the root of female oppression; however, this is a short-sighted viewpoint. The effect and importance of leaders from both sexes on shaping the role of women in the culture and communities of the 21st century will be more efficacious for women and girls than pitting the sexes against one another in a zero-sum game. While the UN Women (2023) "recognizes that women and girls play a vital role as agents of change for sustainable development," it is important to work together with men and remember that the end goal is not power but "ending poverty in all its forms and dimensions everywhere and ensuring the well-being of all" (p. 1-2). In this age of digitization, education becomes the key to achieving gender equality and empowerment of all women and girls.

Social Empowerment through Education

The [UN Women's] Commission recognizes that, despite gains in providing access to education, girls are still more likely than boys to remain excluded from education. It also recognizes that among the gender-specific barriers to girls' equal enjoyment of their right to education are the feminization of poverty, child [labor] undertaken by girls, child, early and forced marriage, female genital mutilation, early and repeat pregnancies, all forms of gender-based violence, including sexual violence and harassment on the way to and from and at school, in their technology-mediated environment, the lack of safe and adequate sanitation facilities, including for menstrual hygiene management, the disproportionate share of unpaid care and domestic work performed by girls and gender stereotypes and negative social norms that lead families and

communities to place less value on the education of girls
than that of boys and may influence the decision of
parents to allow girls to attend school (UN Women,
2023, p. 6)

The role of family and faith communities in building self-
efficacy in women through education cannot be understated.
Family and faith are the cornerstones of society. Unfortunately,
many times faith communities are resistant to innovation. "The
digital divide can ... be influenced by network effects arising
through membership in religious, cultural, economic, and other
communities" (Forenbacher et al., 2019). In the West,
Christianity has been the dominant faith, and it is important to
recognize the resistance it has championed when it comes to
technological innovation. After the printing press made its debut
in 1439, the church in 1515 declared that it had "'brought
untold blessings to mankind'; it was an invention uniquely
advantageous 'to extending the glory of God, to the increase of
the faith, and the diffusion of the arts and sciences'" (Penner,
2012). However, there was also opposition to it by many clergy,
feeling that to allow the common man access to the Scripture
was casting pearls before swine. With the invention of the
television, the church was once again divided. Many in the
church suggested that television was a tool of Satan. Then in the
mid-1950s, a surprising number of educators and parents in the
United States thought that television might reduce educational
unfairness associated with race and poverty. In 1969, Sesame
Street debuted, with the goal of using television to prepare
disadvantaged kids for school. It became the world's most
widely viewed children's television show (Guthrie, 2019). With
the invention of the computer, many in the Christian community

said that science had crossed the line and condemned its use. However, the great scientific minds of the past, such as George Washington Carver, Boyle, Keppler, Maxwell, Newton, and Pascal, were just a few of the many scientists who believed that they could better know their Creator by discovering the laws underlying His creation. Computer scientists can make a similar claim. Computing is a part of God's creation and is meant to serve humanity, though humanity is not free to abuse it. Digitalization of education provides a way for poor and rural communities to access education in ways that have been impossible until now. It is important for communities of faith to embrace technology to fight against injustice and poverty.

In Tanzania, 40% of girls are married before they are 18-years-old with some as young as 11. This explains why 18% of women have no formal education, even though women comprise 51% of the population (Advancing gender, 2019). In 2015, Tanzania enacted the Education Amendment Act, "which issues punishment of up to 30 years for anybody who impregnates a school girl or has sexual relations with one" (Advancing gender, 2019). The government did its part, and yet the problem persists. In Nigeria, 60% of girls are "out-of-school" even though there is a "strong relationship between increased education for girls and lower rates of child marriage, higher incomes and increased decision-making power in the household" (Bakare, 2022). So, the question is, why, with all of the knowledge we have about the importance of women's education, does the problem persist? It is a misunderstanding of the importance of women in culture.

This problem is as old as time and is present in every culture. Hamon (2022), quoting Ramaya states,

> Hindu widows were burnt alive with their husbands' corpses. Japanese men introduced their wives as "my stupid wife." Chinese men said, "it is better to see my son's backside than to see my daughter's face." Believers in reincarnation hold that [being born a woman] is a curse and punishment. A major world religion [considers] women as sex-objects without souls, only to be enjoyed then discarded (p. 125).

Even traditional Jewish teachings from the Talmud encouraged Pharisees to pray daily, "I thank you, God, that I am not a Gentile, a slave, or a woman" (Hamon, 2022, p. 125). When Jesus came, he elevated women in ways that had never been done before. He spoke with them (John 4:5-30), allowed them to touch him (Mark 5:21-34), and spent time teaching them (Luke 10:24-27, *English Standard Version Bible*, 2001/2013). Additionally, women funded his ministry (Luke 8:1-3, *English Standard Version Bible*, 2001/2013). Furthermore, women were essential at the beginning of the church, as seen in Prisca (Romans 16:3), Phoebe (Romans 16:1-2), and numerous other women throughout the New Testament. It is unfortunate to realize that because of a misunderstanding of several passages in the New Testament, women were once again subject to oppression as Western Civilization grew. One of the reasons for this animosity between the genders is the approach of a zero-sum game, where for one gender to succeed, the other must fail. One of the passages generally used to oppress women from the New Testament is 1 Timothy 2:11-12, "Let a woman learn quietly with all submissiveness. I do not permit a woman to teach or to exercise authority over a man; rather, she is to remain quiet" (*English Standard Version Bible*, 2001/2013). First and most importantly is the often-overlooked command in the first four words of the verse: "let a woman learn!" Women's education is non-negotiable from a biblical point of view. Unpacking the entirety of this Scripture is beyond the scope of this paper; however, the word translated as "authority" is interesting. The Greek word *authentein* means "to dominate, usurp, to take control; associated with violence or even murder" (Hamon, 2022, p. 97). It was not a matter of having authority but rather how the authority was enacted, and the reverse is also true. Men are not to dominate, usurp, etc., women either, but rather, "in humility count others more significant than yourselves" (Philippians 2:3, *English Standard Version Bible*, 2001/2013). In a biblical worldview, neither sex should dominate but rather should work in partnership to elevate society.

This is a paradigm shift for much of the global south as it was throughout Western civilization's development. It will take strong leaders from both genders to model this. A study was done in Saudi Arabia to determine what had the greatest impact on women's empowerment. All of the women who participated in the study were educated and ran small businesses. Most studies approach this problem with a preconceived idea that the only solution is government intervention. Even the UN Women's Commission (2023) fell into that trap:

> It stresses the need to recognize and adopt measures to
> reduce, redistribute and value unpaid care and domestic

work by promoting the equal sharing of responsibilities between women and men within the household and by prioritizing, inter alia, sustainable infrastructure, social protection policies and accessible, affordable and quality social services, including care services, childcare and maternity, paternity or parental leave (p. 6).

The study by Al-Rashdi & Abdelwahed (2022) proved that even though men primarily head Saudi households,

[w]omen are fully supported by their families, and their marital relations also improved or became substantial rather than creating any disturbances in their marital status. In other words, female participation in enterprises did not devastate or affect their personal or married life. Moreover, their family members helped them in every walk of life, along with their organizational matters.

These families had learned to work together across gender differences and empower women without sacrificing family. This study goes a long way to underscore the power of a unified approach to poverty alleviation through women's empowerment. It is also essential that the support structures within families undergird the self-efficacy of the women, which is accomplished through education. "Education is essential to boost women's empowerment through generating revenue and self-esteem" (Al-Rashdi & Abdelwahed, 2022).

Modeling plays a critical role in expanding a vision for the role of women in culture. The more women are seen operating as entrepreneurs, doctors, judges, and in other significant societal roles; the more the young women will adopt a self-efficacious attitude. Without models, women have to overcome cultural stereotypes and perceived inefficacy. According to Bandura (1997), "self-limitation arises more from perceived inefficacy than … actual inability" (p. 432). This is seen when considering STEM education. Young girls are often charged with being incapable of math. "Because mathematics is sex-typed as a masculine activity, women harbor a lower sense of mathematical efficacy than do men even when they do not differ in actual math ability" (Bandura, 1997, p. 432). It is important for families to encourage young girls to embrace mathematics in addition to other STEM subjects to compete in the 21st Century's global economy. Focusing on what girls do well instead of ingrained stereotypes is crucial in building efficacy in STEM subjects. Additionally, finding cultural role models for them to follow is an effective way to encourage young girls in this area. When heads of households, be they, men or women, embrace education and technology, they have "a strong, significant, and positive impact in improving the [acceptance of new technology] among rural women of Bangladesh" (Rahman et al., 2021).

Political Empowerment through Education

[The UN Women's Commission intends] to promote and respect the right to education for women and girls throughout the life course and at all levels, especially for those who have been left furthest behind, and address gender disparities, including by investing in public education systems and infrastructure, eliminating discriminatory laws and practices, providing universal access to inclusive, equal and non-discriminatory quality education, including free and compulsory primary and secondary education, promoting lifelong learning opportunities for all, eliminating female illiteracy and promoting financial and digital literacy, ensuring that women and girls have equal access to leadership training, career development, scholarships and fellowships; strive to ensure the completion of early childhood, primary and secondary education and expand vocational and technical education for all women and girls, and foster, as appropriate, intercultural and multilingual education for all; and address negative social norms and gender stereotypes in education systems ... Create conditions for gender-responsive digital learning environments for girls and women who have missed out on education, including by investing in school infrastructure, the development of free, safe and accessible digital public learning resources, with good-quality, multilingual and context-relevant educational content, and the training of teachers to use gender-responsive blended and hybrid learning methods and deliver digital skills training (UN Women, 2023, p. 11)

The most impactful way governments can promote education for women and girls is through infrastructure development. For example, women in rural South Africa have not fully embraced Information Communication Technology (ICT) because of poor network coverage. It is imperative that governments focus on building a technical environment that affords easy access to ICT. Unfortunately, basic service delivery, especially in rural areas of the Global South, is not a top priority. "Despite significant progress in [ICTs], rural dwellers of Bangladesh are still less fortunate when it comes to availing the improved ICT facilities compared to their urban counterparts, and this digital divide is more evident in the case of women" (Rahman et al., 2021). One important "instrument of development, especially in remote and poverty-stricken regions" is mobile phones (Rahman et al., 2021). In fact, "an increase in GDP per capita by 0.9-1.2 percentage points in developing countries can be attained if mobile phone penetration increases to 10 mobile phones per 100 people" (Rahman et al., 2021). The penetration of mobile phones in Nigeria, for example, was "46% in 2016 and 64% in 2017, leading them to classify the country as 'underpenetrated,' [compared] to other countries in the sub-Saharan region such as Kenya (87%), South Africa (84%), and Ghana (74%)" (Forenbacher et al., 2019). Mobile devices are very popular, especially among young people throughout the developing world, and can "serve as a 'bridge' across the digital divide and accelerate economic growth in developing countries" (Forenbacher et al. 2019). In Bangladesh, barriers to mobile phone ownership include poor customer service and poor overall service, which supports the notion that "closing the digital divide requires taking a holistic approach that includes analysis of electricity infrastructure" (Forenbacher et al., 2019). A key driver of mobile phone ownership in Nigeria, for example, is the type of electricity available to the user,

> which is an important finding given that this variable has been neglected in most studies of the digital divide in developing countries. Access to electricity supplied by a generator ... or through a main electricity grid ... was associated with a significantly higher likelihood of

owning a mobile phone, which is consistent with a link between the digital divide and access to a stable electricity supply (Forenbacher et al. 2019).

Those households with reliable electricity connectivity are likelier to embrace ICT, including a network, and to own a mobile device than those without one. Studies prove that "limited electricity can make it difficult for communities to adopt certain ICT tools, and continuous electricity supply is needed to power the technologies, … hence a holistic approach that includes upgrading the electricity infrastructure must be ensued" (Rahman et al., 2021). Many governments have the best intentions of mitigating the digital divide through policy implementation however, often, the data sampling methods provide skewed results that hinder the implementation of national telecommunication policies in the developing world. The good news is that the "urban environment is associated with a narrower digital divide because individuals have easier and cheaper access to ICT and supporting technology, and the costs of adopting ICT infrastructure fall as the population grows and ICT penetration increases" (Forenbacher et al., 2019). This gives hope to rural communities as well.

Another way that governments can facilitate education for women and girls is to empower educational entrepreneurs to play a role by eliminating the bureaucratic hindrances to out-of-the-box solutions for educational development. Bureaucracy is a major barrier to education. In her seminal work, *The Origins of Totalitarianism*, Hannah Arendt (1968) explains, "bureaucracy is always a government of experts, of an 'experienced minority' which has to resist as well as it knows how the constant pressure from the 'inexperienced majority'" (p. 214). The developing world needs to embrace educational entrepreneurship to combat the bureaucratic maze of public education. Innovation takes place at the margins. Schools in the 21st Century must be designed for the information age, not the industrial age, which means focusing on developing digital literacy. In South Africa, for example, women's digital literacy can enhance women's lives and build their self-efficacy. Allowing educational entrepreneurs the freedom to establish "literacy schools and incorporating digital skills in primary and secondary schools in rural municipalities is crucial for empowering women and girls with the needed skills" (Shava, 2021, 17914). The joy of teaching returns with educational choice, whereas bureaucracy destroys that joy. In his book *Great Schools: Global Lessons for High-Caliber, Low-Cost Education*, James Tooley (2022) spells out seven lessons of educational entrepreneurship in no particular order. First, he advocates for "chains" or "brand names" to alleviate the problem for parents of choosing a good school for their children. Additionally, chains can combat teacher retention issues and encourage investment in technology and innovation. Second, those working in the educational, entrepreneurial space must remember that "low cost" for one family will mean "luxury" for the next. Tooley (2022) went to Liberia to explore the development of a private school in the area. He was surprised to have found one already up and running in the town of Monrovia. When asked why children attended that school instead of the free one run by the government, parents answered, "sometimes the government schools [are] full [and] … teachers in public school don't pay full-time attention with the children" (p. 33). Third, to keep the schools affordable to most families, teachers may be paid less than their public school counterparts. This, however, does not automatically mean that they are less qualified or less experienced.

> It may be that those who are more experienced, who have been in the education system longer, develop bad habits, making them less effective in the classroom than teachers who are new and unqualified; more experienced teachers may be increasingly bored with teaching or may have acquired bad habits from being in a low-performing government system (Tooley, 2022, p. 101).

The aforementioned attitude of the Liberian teachers is a case in point. The accountability that these schools have to parents can offset these concerns. Schools can train less experienced educators to compensate for the initial lack of skills. Fourth, Tooley (2022) developed a "sachet economy" approach to education in Ghana because "the cash flow of the poor is daily" (p. 105). In discussing the viability of private education with local parents, he found they were often faced with hidden expenses, such as uniforms, books, PTA, exam fees, etc. These expenses were cost-prohibitive for these families, so Tooley (2022) developed "the idea of an all-inclusive daily fee to cover these eventualities … we amortized the cost of a school uniform, a schoolbag, books, and so on over the whole year and divided the payment by the number of days" (p. 105). Fifth, all educational institutions, whether public or private, face the problem of differentiated learning. This can be alleviated by a subject mastery approach as opposed to a "grade-level" approach and can more easily be addressed in smaller learning environments. Sixth, educational entrepreneurs must grapple with the question of for-profit versus nonprofit. Tooley (2022) provides two examples of nonprofit chains of schools: "a huge chain run by BRAC (Bangladesh Rural Advancement Committee) in Bangladesh… and PEAS (Promoting Equality in African Schools) in Uganda" (p. 109). He also provides guidance for those educational entrepreneurs who prefer the for-profit structure. Finally, his seventh point is whether to buy and build an existing building or build a new one. This will be best answered by the specific community that is served by the educational enterprise. "Investing in digital literacy for women is of paramount importance towards [attaining Sustainable Development] Goal 5…although progress is slow in local municipalities" (Shava, 2021, 17911). Allowing educational entrepreneurs to address digital literacy effectively empowers women to embrace the digital economy and is an effective workaround for local municipalities that are encumbered by educational and governmental bureaucracy. "Literacy education … remains the key to empowering women participation in ICTs towards achieving [Sustainable Development Goal] 5" (Shava, 2021, p. 17913).

Economic Empowerment through Education

The [UN Women's] Commission expresses concern about the unequal pace of digital transformation and the structural and systemic barriers preventing women and girls from being equipped with the knowledge, awareness and skills to leverage connectivity for their economic and social empowerment and to be connected at a level that allows a safe and productive online experience at an affordable cost (p. 3).

Once the governmental hurdles are set aside, economic development becomes possible. The economies of the Global South need women's involvement to unlock their full potential, especially in the area of technology. "There is a positive relationship between economic empowerment and women use of ICT" (Shava, 2021, p. 17910). Unfortunately, "gender inequality is deeply entrenched in our global culture, perpetuating the barriers that exist to full inclusion, digital or otherwise" (Jones, 2019, p. 24). It is ridiculous to think that excluding half of a society will not harm the economic growth of that society. In Saudi Arabia, for example, "women's involvement in the public domain, economy, and employment sector ... has been seen as a revolution in fighting poverty and in boosting Saudi Arabia's Gross Domestic Product (GDP)" (Al-Rashdi & Abdelwahed, 2022). Globally, women are less likely to own mobile phones or have access to the Internet. This access is the first step toward creating "an inclusive digital economy and society" (Jones, 2019, p. 25). Women have been absent in the workforce in much of the Global South. Their participation will require a cultural mindset shift so that "ICTs can be used effectively to empower women in various ... projects such as agriculture, education and small business development" (Shava, 2021, p. 17913). Women must be given "fair opportunity and equal education to participate in the ICT sector, which is crucial for women empowerment" (Shava, 2021, p. 17910).

Another form of discrimination is "refusing women access to finance for purchasing ICT gadgets" (Shava, 2021, p. 17912). This can be alleviated through microfinance loans. Al-Rashdi & Abdelwahed (2022) state that "microfinance plays a considerable and valuable role in women's empowerment." For thousands of years, various charities have been involved in poverty alleviation in Asia and Europe; however, "these financial inclusion models proved insufficient to stem the tide of poverty in what was still known as the 'third world' in 1970" (History of Microfinance, 2017). It was not until the early 1970s, when Muhammad Yunus, an economics professor from Bangladesh, gave a personal loan to a group of 42 women in the village of Jobra to help them start a business, that the concept of microfinance took root. The women repaid the loan, and after approaching multiple banks with the concept (all of which refused), Yunus began Grameen. Grameen

> offered small loans to poor populations, with no financial guarantees required in return. It also ushered in the principle of joint responsibility, which involves solidarity between the members of beneficiary groups. Finally, the program targeted women who had been traditionally excluded from the financial system (History of Microfinance, 2017).

Grameen has flourished since its founding and spurred the development of many other microfinance organizations worldwide. One way that Grameen has successfully used technology is through a partnership with Intel to combat Bangladesh's infant and maternal health crisis. Starting with a pilot program, they began by screening at-risk mothers in rural areas of the country to mitigate nutritional problems during pregnancy. "The ultimate goal is an IT-based product/service combination that can be used by a local entrepreneur to provide a social benefit to the people of Bangladesh" (Yunus, 2010, p. 178). These entrepreneurs would be drawn from "Grameen ladies" (borrowers from the Grameen bank) and "Grameen's New Entreprencurs (GNEs)," who are "the children of Grameen borrowers who have gone through higher education with help from student loans provided by Grameen Bank" (Yunus, 2010, p. 178). The economic impact of microfinance is astonishing; however, even more amazing is how agency has grown in the women who have benefited from the model.

> The jobs for women in ...rural off-farm microenterprises; a new spirit of women's rights and independence and empowerment; dramatically reduced rates of child mortality; rising literacy of girls and young women; and, crucially, the availability of family planning and contraception have made all the difference for these women (Sachs, 2005, p. 14)

The success of Grameen depended on creating a parallel culture for women within the village. "Many women in the villages had never even touched money; some were actually afraid to enter a world they viewed as the exclusive province of men" (Yunus, 2010, p. 65). Grameen began by teaching them to read and write their names, "an incredibly empowering experience for them" (Yunus, 2010, p. 65). These women began coming to the Grameen centers and developed a sense of community among themselves. These communities empowered women to become self-reliant and resourceful. The criticism leveled against

41

Grameen for destroying culture is unfounded. Yunus (2010) explains,

> When people hide behind a culture, you know that's a dead culture, which is good for a museum but not good for human society. To experience progress, human society needs to move on, evolving and creating its own culture step by step. We defied the dead culture in favor of a live culture that is dynamic and self-regenerating (p. 66)

Discrimination must be resisted in all forms for women to participate in the national economy. According to UN Women (2023), gender equality has not yet been achieved, and consequently, women are underrepresented "in all aspects of decision-making, affecting their rights and opportunities in the digital age and being unable to benefit from the millions of decent and quality jobs created by the digital transitions" (p. 5). This in no way means excluding men or competing for power with men. As previously stated, no one wins when men and women are pitted against each other instead of working together for poverty alleviation and justice. "This zero-sum view, where one person's gain is another's loss, ignores the fact that the quality of a workforce significantly impacts a nation's economic vitality" (Bandura, 1997, p. 187). Preparing young girls to enter the economic life of a village will not be easy, as demonstrated in the development of Grameen. However, it is crucial that this happens early in their education. "Young adults forgo vocations they see as providing valued benefits and rewards if they believe they lack the efficacy to fulfill the entry requirements and occupational demands" (Bandura, 1997, p.

189). For this reason, exposing girls to STEM subjects at an early age have the potential to instill the requisite efficacy to enter into those fields as adults. It is much more difficult to reskill adults than to skill children initially. Women invest in the future by investing in their families. This is why it is important for women to become players in the economic development of their country.

Psychological Empowerment through Education

> The [UN Women's] Commission further condemns technology-facilitated gender-based violence and the emergence of new harmful forms of societal narratives which undermine women's online expression, forcing women and girls to self-censor, de-platform or reduce their interaction in online spaces, limiting their participation in public life and the enjoyment of human rights. (p. 5).

The atmosphere of the 21st Century Internet is riddled with censorship. Freedom of speech, which has been the cornerstone of free societies, is being challenged in the name of protecting individuals from "hate speech." The Foundation for Individual Rights and Expression (n.d.) provide three compelling reasons to guard the sanctity of the freedom of speech. First, pursuing knowledge "requires the competition of multiple perspectives." Even if the perspectives are false, it encourages people "to think critically rather than accepting whatever idea is handed to them." Next, "silencing offensive speech can unintentionally give more attention to the speaker." This was demonstrated in

2015, when Milo Yiannopolos became a "free speech martyr" even though his words were "indefensible even to his most vehement fans." Finally, "free speech is necessary for self-government." The free exchange of ideas is vital for a democratic government to operate. Women who are new to this environment must develop a certain level of resilience to wade through the noise. Educators have an obligation when introducing the Internet to students to provide tools with which to navigate the process. Unfortunately, "the use of ICTs by women becomes minimal as women are afraid of being judged" (Shava, 2021, p. 17912). Developing resiliency and critical thinking skills are paramount in this environment.

In her article, "Classroom Culture Promotes Academic Resiliency," Gina DiTullio (2014) encourages teachers to create a classroom environment that facilitates resiliency. She argues that "classroom culture directly affects the teacher's ability to develop [student resiliency]" (DiTullio, 2014, p. 37). She defines resiliency as the ability to "bounce back" after difficulty. DiTullio characterizes resilient students as being able to succeed despite unfavorable conditions, being optimistic, not easily deterred if they don't succeed, understanding that failure is part of learning, having positive self-esteem, a thick skin, and a good sense of humor. She concludes the article with positive steps to create a classroom environment that facilitates resilience. Resilience is a critical skill for adults and is often confused with perseverance. According to Peterson (2023), resilience is a trait, and perseverance is an action. Peterson (2023) characterizes resilience as a type of recovery or adaptation, not a return to the status quo, alluded to by DiTullio (2014, p. 38). Adults can develop both traits, which are cultivated in a "growth mindset" (Peterson, 2023). Peterson considers resilience and perseverance as skills developed through experience. For this reason, when the Internet is first introduced to women, educators should model critical thinking and use discussion techniques to develop these skills in their students. This leads to personal growth for the women. John Maxwell (2018), in his book, *Developing the Leader Within You 2.0*, states, "personal growth increases hope. It teaches us that tomorrow can be better than today" (p. 208). Teachers have a responsibility to model the behavior they want to see. If educators embrace a growth mindset, students will see that although it starts as a seed, it soon becomes a habit and, through perseverance, produces the fruit of positive change in their lives. Students watch to see what happens when obstacles come or failure comes – teachers and parents who model a growth mindset of resilience and perseverance instill confidence in students that it can be done. Maxwell (2018) goes on to say, "[l]ife begins at the end of our comfort zone. To grow, we must embrace change and learn to become comfortable being uncomfortable" (p. 211).

Resilience is a cornerstone of self-efficacy. "Self-efficacy is the women's inner drive and determination to succeed, since it is the ability or efficacy to deal with multiple tasks through self-confidence" (Al-Rashdi & Abdelwahed, 2022). When teaching technical skills, students must be enabled rather than left dependent on the "help desk." This approach will build efficacy in students. It is also critical in a classroom environment where everything is new that the classroom culture is "safe" and invites risk-taking without ridicule. It is tragic when a classroom environment is emotionally unsafe. Mocking and ridicule scar individuals in ways they sometimes don't even recognize, living in what Brene Brown (2018) describes as "hidden shame" disguised as perfectionism, favoritism, comparison, etc. (p. 131). It is the teacher's responsibility to ensure that the classroom environment at every level is emotionally safe so that risks can be taken without the repercussions of shame. There will always be failure; that is part of life. It comes down to how you view failure. For Thomas Edison, "when a reporter asked, 'how did it feel to fail 1000 times?' [he] replied, 'I didn't fail 1000 times. The light bulb was an invention with 1000 steps'" (Salnick). Encouraging both resilience and perseverance should be a goal of every educator.

Conclusion

> [The UN Women's Commission] (2023) emphasizes the
> need to leverage digital technologies to improve and
> supplement teaching, rather than replace in-person
> education, for women and girls (p. 6).

Women, past and present, have been instrumental in building
society. Through years of struggle, women in the West now
enjoy equal opportunity with men for the most part. My father
(Theresa Willen) always told me I could do anything I set my
mind to. He has always been my greatest cheerleader, and I'm
forever grateful for his encouragement. Having strong
advocates is critical for the future empowerment of women, and
where the men can't or won't step up, it is up to women to
advocate for women. The greatest source of women's
empowerment will always be the family. Strengthening families
is paramount for women to thrive and for societies to flourish.
One of the most effective sources of that strength comes from
communities of faith, especially the Church.

By using the word Church, I do not necessarily mean a
building. According to the *New Dictionary of Cultural Literacy*
(2005), a Church is "a group of Christians; *church* is a biblical
word for 'assembly.'" The Church was given a mandate by
Jesus to "disciple the nations" (Matthew 28:18-20, *English
Standard Version Bible*, 2001/2013). Disciple, in this context,
means to teach or to educate. Women missionaries discussed
earlier in this book, like Hasseltine, Boardman, Stockton,
Moon, and Slessor, were all education champions. As we move
into the digital age, we must grapple with the best way forward

in the education space. Following are some suggested solutions to the educational dilemma that we face.

Truth and Transformation, Global
Truth and Transformation is a global movement dedicated to restoring education back to the church within an ecosystem of veritas and virtue. Inspired by the writings of Vishal Mangalwadi, the movement envisions utilizing community churches as venues to house educational centers throughout the world. Through the Internet, people in the world's most remote regions will have access to some of the greatest minds and be able to take advantage of their classes. Locally, an Academic Pastor will mentor the students one-on-one so that they can become leaders in their villages. This model allows girls to study safely without fear of violence.

Low-Cost, High-Quality Private Schools
James Tooley, in his book, *Really Good Schools: Global Lessons for High-Caliber, Low-Cost Education* (2021), highlights thriving private schools that educational experts deny exist. He insists that government-run education is not the savior that many believe it is but rather a behemoth bureaucracy that thwarts real education. He cites many global examples of healthy, thriving schools in places like Sierra Leone, Liberia, and South Sudan. He advocates for educational entrepreneurship that is self-governing and accountable to the families that they serve.

Global Home Education Exchange (GHEX)
Their website states that GHEX is "an international non-governmental organization with a mission to advance, connect, and equip the global home education community." GHEX

stands by the absolute right of every parent to home-educate their children. They are involved in advocacy, outreach, and research serving throughout the world. They provide information about the compulsory education age, the estimated number of people who educate their children at home, and the legal status of home education in many countries worldwide.

There are many other avenues to educate women and girls; we've highlighted only a few. The realization of educating women and girls will require a multi-faceted approach.

Empowering women and girls through education, innovation, and technological change is vital for the alleviation of poverty around the globe. This is done through social, political, economic, and psychological empowerment. Developing self-efficacy in women facilitates a sense of well-being, and "a happy woman is the backbone of national development" (Advancing gender, 2019). Education is the hallmark of achieving this efficacy. Rural areas of the Global South still face daunting barriers to fulfilling educational needs for women and girls; however, through the use of technology, these barriers are becoming more porous. Governmental investment in infrastructure, especially in the area of reliable electricity, will facilitate ICT usage for all. Microfinancing allows women to become entrepreneurs and expedites economic growth. Educational entrepreneurship allows communities to reimagine education and approach it in an unconventional way, encouraging human flourishing and flourishing people lead flourishing communities. Ultimately, efficacious women become leaders and role models in their communities, creating a self-sustaining environment for prosperity.

Mother's Day Proclamation

Arise then…women of this day!

Arise, all women who have hearts!

Whether your baptism *be* of water or of tears!

Say firmly,

"We will not have questions answered by irrelevant agencies,
Our husbands will not come to us, reeking with carnage,
For caresses and applause.

Our sons shall not be taken from us to unlearn all that we have
been able to teach them of charity, mercy and patience.

We, the women of one country, will be too tender of those of
another country to allow our sons to be trained to injure theirs.

From the voice of a devastated Earth a voice goes up with o*ur
own.* It says "Disarm! Disarm!

The sword of murder is not the balance of justice.

Blood does not wipe our dishonor,

nor violence *indicate* possession.

As men have often forsaken the plough and the anvil
at the summons of war, let women now leave all that
may be left of home *For a great and earnest day of counsel.*

Let them meet first, as women, to bewail and commemorate the dead.

Let them solemnly take counsel with each other as to the means whereby the great human family can live in peace…

Each bearing after his own time the sacred impress, not of Caesar, but of God.

In the name of womanhood and humanity, I earnestly ask
that a general congress of women without limit of nationality,
may be appointed and held at someplace deemed most
convenient and the earliest period consistent with its objects,
to promote the alliance of the different nationalities,
the amicable settlement of international questions,
the great and general interests of peace."

Julia Ward Howe, 1870

References

Advancing gender equality. (2019, September 7). *The Citizen; Dar es Salaam.*

Al-Rashdi, N. & Abdelwahed, N. (2022). The empowerment of Saudi Arabian women through a multidimensional approach: The mediating roles of self-efficacy and family support. *Sustainability 2022,* 14, 16349.

Arendt, H. (1968). *The origins of totalitarianism.* Mariner Books.

Bakare, O. (2022, October 14). *Why the girl-child should be up-skilled.* The Guardian Nigeria News. https://headtopics.com/ng/why-the-girl-child-should-be-up-skilled-the-guardian-nigeria-news-nigeria-and-world-news-30713906

Bandura, A. (1997). *Self-efficacy: The exercise of control.* W.H. Freeman and Company.

Brown, B. (2018). *Dare to lead.* Random House.

Cannon, M. (2020). *About.* Mae Cannon. https://maecannon.com/about/

DiTullio, G. (2014) Classroom culture promotes academic resiliency. *Phi Delta Kappa International, 96*(2) 37–40.

English Standard Version Bible. (2013). Harvest House Publishers. (Original work published 2001)

Finlayson, M. (2021, August 9). *Nalini Jayasuriya.* OMSC. https://omsc.ptsem.edu/artist-jayasuriya/

REFERENCES

Forenbacher, I., Husnjak, S., Cvitic, I. & Jovovic, I. (2019). Determinants of mobile phone ownership in Nigeria. *Telecommunications Policy 43*(7). https://doi.org/10.1016/j.telpol.2019.03.001

Grabe, S. & Dutt, A. (2020). Community intervention in the societal inequity of women's political participation: The development of efficacy and citizen participation in rural Nicaragua. *Journal of Prevention & Intervention in the Community 2020, 48*(4), 329-347.

Guthrie, M. (2019, February 6). *50 Years of sunny days on 'Sesame Street': Behind the scenes of TV's most influential show ever.* The Hollywood Reporter. https://www.hollywoodreporter.com/movies/movie-features/sesame-street-turns-50-how-a-childrens-show-revolutionized-television-1183031/

Hamon, J. (2022). *The Deborah company.* Destiny Image Publishers.

Hildreth, L. (2019, February 5). *Missionaries you should know: Betsey Stockton.* IMB.

History of microfinance: Small loans, big revolution (2017, August 17). *BNP Paribas.* https://group.bnpparibas/en/news/history-microfinance-small-loans-big-revolution

Jones, C. (2019). *Achieving gender equality in the age of digital interdependence.* Diplomatic Courier. Retrieved 24, February 2023 from https://www.diplomaticcourier.com/posts/achieving-gender-equality-in-the-age-of-digital-interdependence

Judson, E. C. E. (1860). *Missionary Biography. the memoir of Sarah B. Judson, member of the American Mission to*

REFERENCES

Burmah. by Fanny Forester (miss Emily C. or rather, E. E. Chubbuck). with an introductory notice, by Edward Bean Underhill. T. Nelson & Sons.

Knowles, J. D. (1846). *Memoir of Ann H. Judson: Missionary to Burmah.* BiblioLife.

Littlewood, D. (2022, March 4). *Missionary who went to live with tribe who speared her husband to death.* New Life Publishing.

Macdonald, M. (2018, March 7). *Tanzania: Trailblazer Hilda Kabia is first woman to lead Msalato Theological College.* Episcopal News Service. https://www.episcopalnewsservice.org/2016/06/06/tanzania-trailblazer-hilda-kabia-is-first-woman-to-lead-msalato-theological-college/

Maxwell, J. (2018). *Developing the leader within you 2.0.* Harper Collins Leadership.

Mueller, J. T. (1941). *Mary Slessor (1848-1915).* Missionary Biographies.

Patrao, A & McIntyre, T. (2020). Barriers against safer sex as predictors of condom negotiation self-efficacy among Mozambican women. *European Journal of Public Health,* 20. Supplement 5.

Penner, J. (2012, October 27). The printing press and religion: A study in reciprocity. *ETEC540:Text, Technologies – Community Weblog.* https://blogs.ubc.ca/etec540sept12/2012/10/27/the-printing-press-and-religion-a-study-in-reciprocity/

Peterson, J. (2023). Resilience vs. perseverance: What's the difference? *Think Positive.* Retrieved 7 January 2023 from https://thinkpositivecheck.com/resilience-vs-perseverance-whats-the-difference/.

Pettinger, T. (2019, March 6). *Biography of mother Teresa*. Biography Online. https://www.biographyonline.net/nobelprize/mother_teresa.html

Pioneers. (2022, November 22). *More women in missions: Four reasons why*. Pioneers.

Rahman, M., Ara, T., & Chakma, R. (2021). Explaining geospatial variation in mobile phone ownership among rural women of Bangladesh: A multi-level and multidimensional approach. *Telecommunications Policy 46*(2022). https://doi.org/10.1016/j.telpol.2021.102289

Sachs, J. (2005). *The end of poverty: Economic possibilities for our time*. Penguin Books.

Salnick, K. (n.d.). One thousand steps. *One Thousand Steps*. Retrieved 7 January 2023 from https://www.onethousandsteps.org/

Schreiner, O. (2008, August 16). *Dreams*. Guttenberg. https://www.gutenberg.org/files/1439/1439-h/1439-h.htm#link2H_4_0005

Shava, E. (2021). Gender equality in information communication technology (ICT) for attaining sustainable development goal number 5 in South Africa. *Gender & Behaviour 19*(2). 17906-17917.

Schrock, D. (2014). *Lottie Moon: a brief biography*. chrome-extension://efaidnbmnnnibpcajpcglclefindmkaj/http://cgbcbelton.org/wp-content/uploads/2014/09/lottie-moon1.pdf

REFERENCES

Swaner, L., Eckert, J., Ellefsen, E. & Lee, M. (2022). *Future-ready: Innovative missions and models in Christian education.* Association of Christian Schools International and Cardus.

The New Dictionary of Cultural Literacy (2005). Houghton Mifflin Harcourt Publishing Company. Retrieved March 3, 2023, from https://www.dictionary.com/browse/church#:~:text=defini tions%20for%20church-,church,Christians%20living%20in%20the%20world.

The three arguments in support of free speech (n.d.). *Foundation for Individual Rights and Expression.* https://www.thefire.org/research-learn/three-arguments-support-free-speech

Tooley, J. (2021). *Really good schools: Global lessons for high-caliber, low-cost education.* Independent Institute.

UNESCO Institute of Statistics. (2019, December 17). *Literacy.* UNESCO UIS.

UN Women (2022, August 23). *In focus: Sustainable development goal 5.* Retrieved 24 February 2023 from https://www.unwomen.org/en/news-stories/in-focus/2022/08/in-focus-sustainable-development-goal-5#:~:text=The%20achievement%20of%20gender%20equ ality%20is%20the%20fifth%20of%2017,a%20better%20f uture%20for%20all

UN Women (2023). *Commission on the status of women.* https://www.unwomen.org/sites/default/files/2023-02/CSW67%20Agreed%20Conclusions_zero%20draft_1 %20February%202023.pdf

REFERENCES

WorldBank. (n.d.). *Gender Literacy Rates*. World Bank Gender Data Portal. Retrieved February 24, 2023, from https://genderdata.worldbank.org/indicators/se-adt/

Yunus, M. (2010). *Building social business*. Public Affairs.

Author Bios

Teresa Janzen, M.Ed.

Teresa Janzen is the Senior Advisor for Partner Relationships and Strategic Development for ACROSS in Juba, South Sudan. As an author, speaker, and host of the Radical Abundance Podcast, Teresa inspires people to pursue their life's passion relentlessly. She holds a master's degree in Education from West Texas A&M and is currently working on her Doctorate in Ministry at Fuller Seminary with an emphasis on adaptive leadership and change management in a multicultural context.

Theresa Willen, M.Ed.

Theresa Willen is the Executive Director of Truth and Transformation, USA, an organization dedicated to restoring education back to an ecosystem focused on truth and character. An international speaker and published author, Theresa advocates for women's empowerment through education and parental rights in education. She holds a master's degree in Education, with an emphasis on Instructional Design, and is currently working on her Doctorate in Educational Leadership. Her research interest is reimagining the global educational systems to focus on a more holistic approach to liberating the uniqueness of every learner.

www.ingramcontent.com/pod-product-compliance
Lightning Source LLC
Chambersburg PA
CBHW020339130626
46549CB00003B/1215